A History of Britain

BRITAIN IN THE MODERN WORLD

1900–2007

Richard Dargie

FRANKLIN WATTS
LONDON•SYDNEY

First published in 2008 by Franklin Watts

© 2008 Arcturus Publishing Limited

Franklin Watts
338 Euston Road
London NW1 3BH

Franklin Watts Australia
Level 17/207 Kent Street, Sydney, NSW 2000

Produced by Arcturus Publishing Limited,
26/27 Bickels Yard, 151–153 Bermondsey Street, London SE1 3HA

Series concept: Alex Woolf
Editor and picture researcher: Patience Coster
Designer: Phipps Design

Picture credits:
akg-images: 6.
Corbis: cover photo of Tony Blair and George Bush (Reuters), 4 (Hulton-Deutsch Collection), 7 (Hulton-Deutsch Collection), 9 (top, Hulton-Deutsch Collection), 13 (bottom), 14 (top) and cover, 19 and cover (Jose Fuste Raga), 22 (Bettmann), 29 and cover (Haider Al-Assadee/epa).
Corbis/Sygma: 23 (Henri Bureau), 25 (Bradford T&A), 26 (Colin McPherson), 27 and cover (Tim Graham).
Dover: 5.
Getty Images: 21 (Time & Life Pictures), 24 (Hulton Archive).
Mary Evans Picture Library: 16 (Andrew Besley), 17.
The Bridgeman Art Library: 11 (Archives Charmet), 13 (top, ILN Picture Library).

A CIP catalogue record for this book is available from the British Library.

Dewey Decimal Classification Number: 942.082

ISBN 978 0 7496 8198 2

Printed in China

Franklin Watts is a division of Hachette Children's Books.

Contents

The Birth of the Welfare State

In the 20th century, Britain won two world wars but lost its overseas empire. It also became a social democracy, and life for most Britons was transformed after 1950 by new technology and prosperity.

A new generation of radical Liberal MPs, such as David Lloyd George and Winston Churchill who were determined to modernize Britain, came to power in the 1906 election.

Imperial Jubilee

In 1897, colonial troops from every part of the empire paraded through London to mark Queen Victoria's Diamond Jubilee. There was great pride in Britain's overseas empire, which stretched across the globe from Canada to New Zealand. But the celebrations were soon overshadowed by the news of humiliating defeats against the Boers in the war in South Africa. More worrying still was the menacing rise of Germany as a military and industrial rival. Worried by Germany's technical superiority, the Conservative government hurriedly laid the foundation for a national system of secondary schools, so that British youngsters would be as well educated as their German counterparts.

Liberal Landslide

In the 1906 election, the Liberals and their allies won a crushing victory at the polls. Liberal leaders such as David Lloyd George, Winston Churchill and John Burns were radicals who wanted to make Britain a fairer society by helping the millions of poor who were living below the poverty line.

As Churchill argued in 1906, 'the State must now earnestly concern itself with the care of the sick, the aged and children'. This was not simple idealism or charity, for Churchill knew that Britain's industrial rivals, such as the USA and Germany, were better at educating and training their people. Like other politicians at the time, he wanted to improve Britain's 'national efficiency'.

Welfare Britain

The 1906 Liberal government passed a number of important laws to help the weakest in society. Children from poor families were often affected by hunger and illness which prevented them from learning, so school meals and medical inspections were introduced in 1908. To help the elderly poor, a pension for seventy year olds was introduced in 1909 on a sliding scale from one to five shillings per week. Measures were also taken to help injured and unemployed workers, and to assist workers in low-paid trades such as tailoring. The Chancellor, David Lloyd George, also planned a system of national insurance to provide a small income for the sick and unemployed in times of personal difficulty. For the first time, the government accepted that it had a responsibility for the welfare of the British people.

The People's Budget

To fund its reforms, the Liberal government needed to raise an extra £15 million in revenue. Lloyd George's 1909 budget set out plans to do this by taxing the wealthy owners of large estates. The House of Lords resisted these plans, sparking a crisis and a general election. The Liberals won and their budget was passed. In 1911, the Parliament Act gave the Commons more power than the Lords, an arrangement that has continued to the present day.

Many working families had fallen below the poverty line in the Victorian age and child poverty was widespread. The new welfare state aimed to improve conditions for the struggling poor.

1914–18

World War I

During the summer of 1914, Europe slid slowly but inevitably towards a major conflict. The Great War of 1914–18 was unprecedented in scale and cost. It affected not just the men fighting at the Front, but all sections of British society.

War Preparations

Worried by Germany's military and industrial power, Britain had reached 'agreements' with France in 1904 and Russia in 1906. The government established the British Expeditionary Force (BEF) in case Britain needed quickly to deploy an armed force overseas. The Territorial Force and Officers' Training Corps provided future reserves of manpower and leadership. Powerful *Dreadnought* battleships were built in response to Germany's modern North Sea fleet.

Trench Warfare

The German invasion of Belgium forced Britain into war, for it could not accept a hostile presence in the ports directly across the Channel. The BEF was sent to France, but by early December most of its 100,000 men had been killed in the fighting. In 1915, the horrific realities of industrialized war set in: barbed wire, bombardment, poison gas, mines, shell-shock, trench-foot, rats and mud. A new volunteer army responded to Lord Kitchener's call to arms but was savaged in battle at Ypres and Loos. As the war dragged on into 1916, conscription became necessary. Those who died that year at the Somme were later described as 'lions led by donkeys', and the British command was certainly slow to understand the new technologies of war. Nevertheless, the British army which fought the decisive Battle of Amiens in August 1918 was a well-equipped, battle-hardened fighting force, supported by massed tanks and the airpower of the new Royal Air Force (RAF).

Britain was alarmed by the size of Germany's growing North Sea fleet. Based at Wilhelmshaven and Kiel (above), it threatened the Royal Navy's control of Britain's home waters.

Distant Fronts

With stalemate on the Western Front, Churchill suggested striking at Germany's ally, Turkey. However, blunders in executing his daring plan condemned the Australian, New Zealand and British forces to murderous exposure on the beaches of Gallipoli near Istanbul. In the Middle East, British forces eventually wore down Turkish resistance, thanks in part to the charismatic scholar-warrior T. E. Lawrence, who roused the Arabs against their Turkish rulers.

War at Sea and in the Air

The main job of the Royal Navy was to blockade the German fleet. Both sides avoided open sea battle until meeting off Danish Jutland in 1915. British ships took the heavier hits, after which the Germans retreated to their ports. From then on, the Germans tried to cut off Britain's supply of food and raw materials using U-boats (submarines). They were so successful that the British government considered surrendering in 1916. The U-boat menace was finally overcome by the convoy system, helped by technical advances such as hydrophones and depth charges.

The Impact of War

The 1914–18 war affected everyone, even the residents of southern England who suffered in the first air raids. Women worked in munitions factories and served as nurses. Food shortages led to rationing. Country schoolchildren had to work on the farms. Luxuries such as alcohol were restricted. Propaganda posters were everywhere. The war took a million British and Empire lives and cost thirty-five billion pounds. However, it also sponsored astonishing advances in new technologies such as radio and aviation.

Timeline

1904	• Britain makes 'entente', or agreement, with France
1906	• HMS *Dreadnought*, the most powerful battleship of the day, is launched
1914	• Britain enters war to protect Belgian neutrality
1915	• Kitchener's volunteer army is massacred at Ypres and Loos
1915	• Allied attack on Turkey fails at Gallipoli
1916	• Compulsory military conscription is introduced
1918	• British make gains against the Germans in the autumn
1919	• Peace treaty arranged at Versailles near Paris

In the battlefields of France, poisonous chemical gases were used for the first time in the history of warfare. Gas masks were developed in an effort to protect the troops.

Votes for Women

By 1900, the movement for women's suffrage had gained many supporters. While the actions of militant suffragettes after 1903 did not result in progress, women's wartime efforts brought a partial reward in 1918.

New Status

After 1860, divorced women enjoyed increased legal rights, while all married women gained greater control of their property in 1882. After 1872, most British girls attended elementary school and increasing numbers studied at college. Women's political rights also changed. Propertied women gained the right to vote in School Board elections in 1870. After 1884, they could also vote in district elections. Women had begun to participate in Britain's democracy but still had no parliamentary vote. To many, this seemed unjust.

Emmeline Pankhurst, a founder of the Women's Social and Political Union, was repeatedly arrested for militant behaviour. She died in 1928, shortly after women gained the vote on equal terms with men.

Campaigning

Local women's suffrage societies developed in Britain after 1870 and merged into a National Union in 1897. By 1914, the NUWSS (National Union of Women's Suffrage Societies) had a membership of over 100,000 and organized massive street demonstrations. Although its leaders were mainly middle class, the NUWSS recruited members from among the women mill-workers of Lancashire and Lanarkshire. In the 1906 election, it threatened to run its own candidates against unsympathetic men. The Women's Freedom League encouraged its members to withhold payment of their rates and boycott the 1911 census. However, some women formed anti-suffrage societies, arguing in their pamphlets that women were not suited for a life outside the home. These women expressed views that were held by the bulk of British society of both genders at the time.

Suffragette 'Terror'

After 1903, the Women's Social and Political Union (WSPU) began its programme of radical action. The Prime Minister was assaulted on holiday and the Home Secretary was pelted with eggs. Places of male recreation, such as golf courses, football pitches and cricket grounds, were vandalized. Letters in pillar boxes in business and banking areas were destroyed with paraffin and corrosive acids. One suffragette, Emily Davison, even died for her beliefs when she threw herself under the hooves of Anmer, the king's horse in the 1913 Epsom Derby. The government responded by arresting WSPU leaders. Hunger strikers were released to recuperate and re-arrested when stronger. By 1914, the WSPU militants had alienated public opinion and women had still not gained equal voting rights with men.

Women and War

When war came in 1914, many suffragettes backed the war effort, as did most British women of all classes. The WSPU paper *Suffragette* was renamed *Britannia*. Others supported the Women's Peace Crusade. In 1918, the coalition government extended the vote to women over the age of thirty. Equal franchise with men was achieved in 1928.

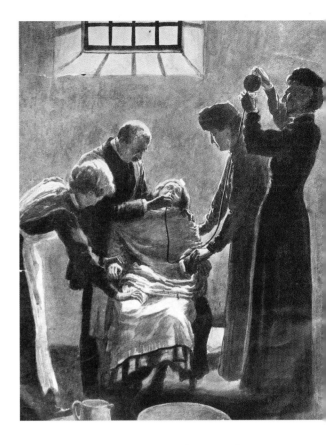

Militant suffragettes who went on hunger strike while in prison were force fed. In 1913, the 'Cat and Mouse Act' was passed. This meant that suffragettes on hunger strike were released from prison when starvation had made them weak, but arrested again once they had recovered.

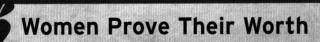

Women Prove Their Worth

Prime Minister Herbert Asquith had been openly opposed to voting rights for women. However, he was so impressed by the zeal with which women worked during World War I that he remarked: 'How could we have carried on the war without them? I find it impossible to withhold from women the power and the right of making their voices directly heard.'

Women's struggle to win equal voting rights with men was much helped by World War I, when women were employed to do 'men's work' on the Home Front.

Slump

After 1919, new technological industries prospered but traditional industries endured years of slump.

David Lloyd George served as an energetic war premier from 1916–18. He was voted back into office in the immediate aftermath of the war by a grateful British public.

A Changing Economy

In 1919, the British economy seemed strong because the war had encouraged new industries such as electronics, aviation and car production. However, thanks to government decisions, these 'industries of the future' were based in southern and central England. The old industrial centres in northern England, Scotland, South Wales and Northern Ireland were busy during the war while demand for coal, iron and textiles was high. However, they were part of the old Victorian economy, and by 1921 many old-fashioned factories in these areas were closing.

Coal Slide

The trade crisis after 1921 led to unemployment and strikes. Working people looked to the Labour Party for leadership, but the Labour governments of 1924 and 1929–31 failed to solve Britain's economic ills. Cheap foreign coal led to a slump in demand for expensive British coal. The government suggested reducing the miners' wages and lengthening their working hours, but the furious miners demanded 'Not a minute on the day, not a penny off the pay.' On 3 May 1926, people in many industries stopped work in a General Strike in support of the miners.

Another Britain

While millions suffered in the slump, skilled workers in the new industries saw the purchasing power of their wages rise. Many working families could afford to install domestic electricity and buy new consumer products such as a 'wireless' or a 'hoover'. In the south and in the Midlands, there was a building boom and thousands of people put down their £10 deposit on a new semi-detached home. There was cash left over from the average weekly wage of £3 to buy luxuries. Trips to the 'pictures' were well within the average budget, although only the middle and upper classes could afford a motor car.

General Strike

The government feared a people's revolution, as in Russia nine years earlier, but the strike only lasted nine days and there were few violent incidents. Volunteers kept some trains and buses running. Although the national newspapers were closed during the strike, the new British Broadcasting Corporation (BBC) transmitted the news and the government kept control of the situation. But the failed strike left bitter memories in many working-class communities.

Depression

A serious stock market slump in the USA (the Wall Street Crash) badly affected Britain and the government devalued the pound in September 1929. Trade slowed to a halt and by 1931 three million were unemployed, mostly in the older industrial areas. Single-industry towns such as shipbuilding Jarrow were badly hit. To limit public spending, the coalition national government introduced the hated 'means test'. The symbol of the Depression was Order 534, the vast ocean liner that sat unfinished on the Clyde for three years.

Crowds of worried investors gather outside the stock exchange in New York, USA, in the chaos of the 1929 Wall Street Crash.

The Road to War

After 1920, Britain was deeply involved in preserving the international peace. However, by the late 1930s the nation was again facing world war.

Peace Issues

After 1920, British governments supported the League of Nations and its attempts to preserve international peace. Setting an example, Britain accepted limits on its fleet in 1922. After 1930 however, Britain and the League failed to stop Japanese aggression in Manchuria or prevent the collapse of the World Disarmament Conference in 1933.

The Italian Threat

In the early 1930s, British leaders were worried by the rise of fascism in Italy and by that country's threat to Britain's influence in the Mediterranean. In 1935, Italy invaded Abyssinia, the last independent African state. The League of Nations imposed sanctions upon Italy, but these excluded oil and other war materials. Although the Italians used poison chemicals against the Abyssinians, the British government allowed Italian ships access to the Suez Canal, in the hope of winning Italy as an ally. French and British foreign ministers devised a plan to give much of Abyssinia to Italy. When the plan was revealed in 1935, it caused a public protest. It also exposed British declarations about the value of the League as just empty words. Europe had returned to traditional 'great power' diplomacy.

Nazi Threat

By 1936, the German leader Adolf Hitler had begun to break the terms of the 1919 Versailles peace settlement. Britain had already agreed to increased German naval strength in 1935. When Hitler illegally remilitarized the Rhineland, many British

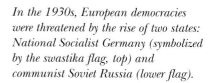

In the 1930s, European democracies were threatened by the rise of two states: National Socialist Germany (symbolized by the swastika flag, top) and communist Soviet Russia (lower flag).

Timeline

1931	• Japanese aggression in Manchuria reveals weakness of League of Nations
1935	• Exposure of British and French plans to allow Italian domination of Abyssinia
1935	• Britain signs naval pact with Nazi Germany
1936	• Hitler re-enters the demilitarized Rhineland
1938	• Hitler annexes Austria
1938	• Britain sacrifices Czechoslovakia at Munich
1939	• Hitler invades Poland

people were unconcerned, believing he had a right to 'enter his own backyard'. France was willing to fight to preserve the 1919 peace, but London valued Hitler as a defence against communist Russia. Hitler's invasion of Austria in 1938 also seemed acceptable, although it broke the Versailles treaty. Nazi intervention in the Spanish Civil War was overlooked too, for many preferred a stable fascist Spain under General Franco to a Spanish republic with links to Russia.

Munich Appeasement

In the late 1930s, British Prime Minister Neville Chamberlain's government appeased Hitler by granting his territorial demands. Chamberlain believed that the British public was opposed to another European war. He also knew that Britain was not ready to fight the Nazis, so he flew three times to Germany to meet Hitler in 1938. At the Munich Conference, Chamberlain succeeded in postponing war in Europe but had to sacrifice democratic Czechoslovakia to German territorial demands.

British Prime Minister Neville Chamberlain, shown here in a cheery pose on the cover of The Sphere *magazine, pursued a policy of appeasement with Hitler.*

Back to War

In March 1939, Hitler illegally annexed the remainder of Czechoslovakia. Appeasement had failed and Chamberlain reluctantly put Britain on a war footing, doubling the Territorial Force and guaranteeing Polish independence from German aggression. When Germany invaded Poland on 1 September, Britain honoured its commitment to the Polish people two days later, and declared war on the aggressor.

German troops march into Poland on 1 September 1939. This action triggered the start of World War II.

World War II

Britain hung on alone in the disastrous early years of the war, but eventually its alliances with Russia and the USA ensured victory.

Blitzkreig

In the first seven months of the war there was little fighting in Western Europe. In April 1940 however, Hitler occupied Denmark and Norway to secure his iron-ore supplies. Winston Churchill replaced Chamberlain as Prime Minister on 10 May 1940, the same day that Hitler launched his *Blitzkrieg* ('lightning war') in the west. With superiority in tanks and aircraft, the German army swept through the Low Countries. British forces were cut off from the French army and retreated towards the port of Dunkirk, where a fleet of small ships braved bombardment to rescue 340,000 stranded British troops. When France surrendered, Britain was left alone to face Germany and fascist Italy.

The Battle of Britain

Before Hitler could invade Britain, he needed supremacy in the air. From July to September 1940, the Luftwaffe and RAF battled for control of the skies above southern England. By mid-September, 730 pilots had been lost but the RAF still controlled the daytime skies. From then on, the Germans concentrated on bombing London and other industrial cities at night. However, British morale and industrial production were quickly restored after air raids, thanks to those who served as rescuers, medical workers and fire fighters.

Global War

In 1941, Britain lost ground in North Africa and the Mediterranean. In the Atlantic, German U-boats were sinking ships carrying essential supplies to Britain.

"NEVER WAS SO MUCH OWED BY SO MANY TO SO FEW" THE PRIME MINISTER

Above and left: the Prime Minister, Winston Churchill, praised the actions of RAF pilots in the Battle of Britain with his famous words: 'Never in the field of human conflict was so much owed by so many to so few.'

However, by the end of the year Britain had two powerful new allies, Russia and the USA, thanks to Hitler's attack on Russia and the Japanese attack on Hawaii. Before Allied fortunes turned, there were further defeats, such as the loss of Singapore, and it took time before sonar and depth charges began to defeat the German U-boat threat. Eventually, however, the Allies won victories in North Africa, Italy and in north-west Europe, while Germany's luck ran out against the Russians on its Eastern Front.

A Nation at War

During World War II, Britain became a centralized state with all planning decided by the government. The civilian population was mobilized, with thousands employed in shipyards, weapons factories or drafted to work in the mines. Scientists used new technologies such as plastics to make cheap parts for aircraft and tanks. British physicists made important contributions to the development of the atomic bomb. The Ministry of Information reminded every Briton of his or her duty to be careful with valuable resources such as coal and food. The welfare reforms suggested in the Beveridge Report of 1942 and the Butler Education Act of 1944 gave British people a glimpse of a better life after eventual victory. Peace came in May 1945, when Churchill declared Victory in Europe to the exhausted but elated British.

Propaganda posters from the Ministry of Information reminded Britons to be resourceful and do their bit to help the war effort.

A triumphant Winston Churchill declared Victory in Europe on 8 May 1945.

Timeline

July–September 1940	• RAF gain the advantage during the Battle of Britain
September 1940	• Hitler postpones his planned invasion of Britain
1940-41	• The Blitz – Germans bomb British cities
June 1941	• Germany attacks Russia
December 1941	• Japan attacks US Navy at Pearl Harbour
May 1942	• Allied fleets begin to win the Battle of the Atlantic
June 1944	• Allied troops land in north-west Europe
May 1945	• Victory in Europe
August 1945	• Victory over Japan

Austerity and Consumerism

After 1945, the Labour government tried to build a welfare state. But prosperity only came with the rise of a new consumer society in the 1950s.

Brave New World

During World War II, many dreamed of a fairer society afterwards. The Labour Party promised that the state would care for the nation 'from the cradle to the grave', and easily won the 1945 election as a result. In 1946, national insurance protection for the sick and unemployed was extended to all adults. Maternity and death grants and national assistance benefit payments helped poorer families to cope. Despite opposition from many doctors, in 1948 Labour created a National Health Service that cared for all, regardless of income.

Nationalization and Shortage

After 1945, Labour nationalized important industries such as power, steel and transport by taking them into government control. However, the products of Britain's factories had to be sold abroad to help reduce the wartime debt. High taxes on luxury goods meant that many British consumers could not afford them. Clothing and many foods remained rationed in Labour's 'command economy'.

The return to normal civilian life and the climate of optimism in the period immediately after the war led to a rise in the birth rate throughout Britain, known as the 'baby boom'.

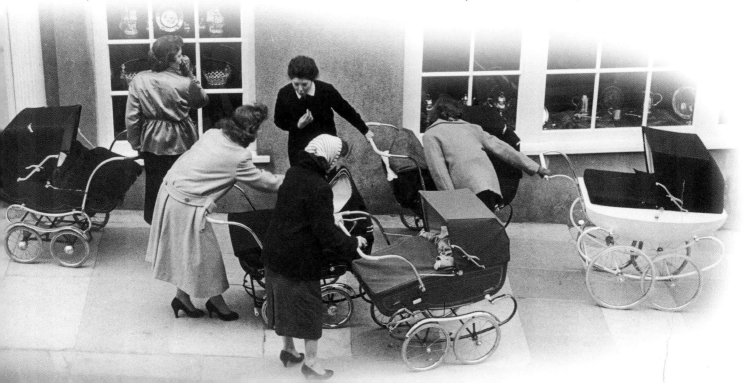

A young woman poses in the driver's seat of an MGB convertible, Britain's best-selling sports car in the postwar years, introduced in 1962.

There were difficulties distributing essentials such as coal. Labour could not solve the housing shortage either, for construction materials were scarce. Despite the postwar 'baby boom', many newlyweds had to move in with relatives. Americans visiting Britain in 1951 found the atmosphere so grim that they thought the country was still at war.

Golden Years?

The age of austerity only began to come to an end in the 1950s. Once back in government, the Conservative Party encouraged industry to set about meeting the needs of domestic consumers. The new medium of television advertising helped in this regard. From 1953 to 1970, unemployment was low, wages increased and living standards improved, especially for many working-class families. Yet there were fundamental problems in the British economy. Poor management, low productivity and strikes hindered British industry. Britain prospered after the war, but was still the 'sick man of Europe'.

The Sixties

By the 1960s, young people in Britain had more money than ever before and wanted to spend it on their own fashions and music. Britain had also become a more tolerant society, with laws against abortion and homosexuality relaxed in 1967. Many young people protested against the Vietnam War, apartheid and the British deployment of nuclear missiles. Horror at the pollution caused by a supertanker disaster off the coast of Cornwall in 1967 helped to promote public interest in environmental conservation.

Car Industry Stalls

By 1975 most consumers could afford a car, yet almost half the cars on British roads were foreign built and the British car industry was in decline. Three of the four main car groups were American-owned, but it was the build quality of European and Japanese imports that posed the greatest threat to British producers. British car plants struggled with old machinery and methods, poor management and an out-of-date trades union structure.

The End of Empire

After 1945, the empire quickly faded away, but Britain found a new future in Europe.

A New World Order

In World War I, Australia, New Zealand and Canada fought alongside Britain. After 1918, these former colonies were given independence but joined the Commonwealth, a body of nations with links to the British Crown. Many Indians had also fought for Britain, but they were only offered limited powers of self-rule. Indian nationalists rebelled against this and over 350 protesters were killed by British troops at Amritsar in 1919. After this massacre, many in Britain agreed with the Indian leader, Mahatma Gandhi, that British rule in India had to end. In 1945, the new Labour government decided to withdraw from India and in August 1947 the states of India and Pakistan were created.

The Indian leader, Mahatma Gandhi, encouraged the tactic of peaceful civil disobedience as a means of gaining independence from British colonial rule.

In Egypt, the nationalist president, Colonel Nasser, took over the Suez Canal in 1956, threatening Britain's communications with the Far East. Together with France and Israel, Britain sent troops into Egypt, provoking international condemnation. The invasion ended in humiliation for British Prime Minister Anthony Eden when the Americans refused to support him. Many British colonies gained their independence in the decade after the Suez Crisis. In 1957, Ghana was the first new black state to emerge in Africa. Britain's days as the world's leading colonial power were over now.

Missed Opportunity

After 1945, several Western European states began to work towards closer co-operation. But Britain still saw itself as a major power that could make its way in the world alone. It also believed that it enjoyed a special relationship with the USA. Britain therefore did not join the European Economic Community of 1957, a common market of over

200 million customers. Instead, Britain's contribution to Europe was made through bodies such as the military alliance, NATO (the North Atlantic Treaty Organization) based at Mons near Brussels.

European Membership

Prime Minister Harold Macmillan realized that Britain's future lay in closer co-operation with Europe, but attempts to join the EEC were blocked by the French in 1963 and 1967. Finally, under Prime Minister Edward Heath, Britain joined the EEC in 1973. By that time, many of the EEC's rules affecting key industries such as farming and fishing were at odds with British practice, and these industries suffered badly. By the 1980s there were many in Britain who feared further integration with Europe. These anti-Europeans looked to Conservative Prime Minister Margaret Thatcher to champion their cause. Thatcher, however, was a realist and signed the 1987 Single European Act which allowed people and goods to flow more freely around Europe. In 1993, anti-Europeans formed a political party, the UK Independence Party (UKIP), which stood for British withdrawal from the European Union. However, UKIP made little impact in elections in 2001 and 2005.

Timeline

1919	• More than 1,600 people are killed or wounded at a massacre at Amritsar in the Punjab
1947	• Creation of India and Pakistan
1956	• Suez Crisis in Egypt
1957	• Ghana gains its independence
1957	• The EEC is established, with just six original member states
1973	• Britain joins the EEC
2007	• The European Union has a total of twenty-seven member states

Britain was a driving force behind the creation of the Council of Europe in 1949 (below) but missed out on the chance to shape the European Community that began in Brussels in 1957.

Thatcher's Britain

Prime Minister Margaret Thatcher reshaped British party politics and the economy by reducing trade union power. Her ruthlessly determined approach earned her the nickname the 'Iron Lady'.

Margaret Thatcher, Prime Minister from 1970 to 1990, became known as the Iron Lady after making clear her firm position on the Cold War in 1976.

Winter of Discontent

The 1970s were years of inflation and rising long-term unemployment. In 1976, the Labour government even had to ask the International Monetary Fund (IMF) for a £2.3 billion loan. The trades unions rejected the government's call for limits on wages and called their members out on strike during the winter of 1978–79. Pickets outside hospitals and rats scuttling in mountains of uncollected rubbish on the streets of London made powerful television and press headlines. The Conservative Party's election poster slogan 'Labour isn't working' helped to sweep Thatcher to power.

Privatization

Margaret Thatcher believed that Britain's decline was the result of the economic foundations laid down by the post-war Labour government. She believed that British people needed to be freed from government control and that public spending had to be curbed. State industries such as British Telecom were privatized. Council houses were sold to tenants at discounted prices to create a 'property owning democracy'. Critics argued that speculators cashed in on these 'sell offs'. Nevertheless, international confidence in Britain strengthened and brought in foreign investment to the London stock market. Inflation was squeezed out of the system but at the cost of high numbers of unemployed and bankrupted firms.

Union-bashing

In 1983, Thatcher won a massive parliamentary majority, thanks to the triumphant public mood after the Falklands War. Now she could take on the unions. The miners had defeated Edward Heath's Conservative government in 1973, but large coal stocks and vast oil and gas reserves from the North Sea gave Thatcher a stronger hand. Violent clashes between police and pickets throughout the year-long strike were recorded in disturbing detail by the media. Eventually the strike collapsed as the men returned to work. Within a year, the British coal industry had largely disappeared and all but fifteen pits were closed. New laws gave ordinary trade union members more of a say in decisions and reduced the influence of extremists. British industry entered a period of calm that attracted foreign investors such as the carmaker Nissan, which opened its successful Sunderland plant in 1986.

Cold Warrior

Nicknamed the Iron Lady by the Soviets, Thatcher was a natural ally of their Cold War rival, US President Ronald Reagan. When the Soviets deployed their long-range nuclear missiles in Eastern Europe, Thatcher permitted the USA to site their Tomahawk Cruise missiles on British soil, despite protests by peace campaigners such as the Greenham Common women. She was, however, quick to appreciate the significance of President Mikhail Gorbachev's attempts to reform the Soviet Union through *glasnost* (openness) and *perestroika* (restructuring). One of the longest serving prime ministers, she was still in power as the Cold War ended and claimed to have played an important role in helping to bring about the Soviet downfall after 1989.

A pensioner demonstrates against Margaret Thatcher's 'community charge' or 'poll tax'. The poll tax (a tax on individuals) was introduced to replace the rates (a tax on property) and was deeply unpopular.

Timeline

1975	• Margaret Thatcher replaces Edward Heath as Conservative Party leader
1979	• Conservatives win general election after the 'winter of discontent'
1982	• Britain wages war against Argentina over possession of the Falkland Islands
1984-85	• Thatcher takes on and defeats the National Union of Mineworkers
1989	• The 'poll tax' is introduced in Scotland
1990	• Thatcher resigns from office after failing to win support from her Cabinet

Irish Independence

In the 20th century, Ireland witnessed armed uprising, civil war and a bitter partition that split the island into two separate states.

Ireland Under Arms

When the Liberal government tried to steer a Home Rule Bill through Parliament in 1912–13, Protestant Ulster Unionists pledged to resist Dublin rule. The Unionist leader, Sir Edward Carson, got together a force of 80,000 armed supporters. Irish nationalists retaliated by forming the Irish Volunteers. The British government could not rely on its forces to maintain order, for many officers were Unionist sympathizers. As Ireland faced up to civil war, events there were overshadowed by the outbreak of a great European war.

Easter 1916

During World War I, radical groups such as the Irish Republican Brotherhood saw a chance to overthrow British rule by force. In Easter 1916, republicans took control of key points in central Dublin and announced the creation of an independent Irish republic. Despite being outgunned, they held out for six days. The British military executed sixteen republicans, including their wounded leader, James Connolly, who was strapped to a chair in front of the firing squad. Nationalist Ireland was appalled by the treatment of the '1916 martyrs', and support for their cause contributed to the overwhelming electoral victory of the republican party, Sinn Fein (Ourselves Alone), two years later.

Sinn Fein volunteers in uniform on the first day of the revolt of Easter 1916.

Timeline

1914	• Home Rule Bill passed but postponed by outbreak of WWI
1916	• Easter Rising in Dublin
1918	• Sinn Fein wins election in Ireland
1919-21	• IRA wages guerrilla war against the British
1922	• Partition of Ireland comes into effect
1967-68	• Beginning of 'the Troubles' in Northern Ireland
1969	• British troops are sent to Northern Ireland
1972	• Thirteen people are killed on 'Bloody Sunday'
1994	• Ceasefire declared by the IRA and its opponents

War and Partition

Sinn Fein set up a separate Parliament in Dublin while the Irish Republican Army (IRA) waged guerrilla war from 1919 to 1921. The British responded by using forces such as the brutal Black and Tans. The Irish war was soon reduced to a bloody round of atrocities and acts of retaliation, but the desire of most Irish people for independence was clear. In the May 1921 elections, Sinn Fein won every seat outside Ulster apart from one. Prime Minister Lloyd George suggested the solution of partitioning Ireland. Ulster Unionists were happy to remain in Britain, while many nationalists accepted the loss of Ulster as a temporary price to pay for peace and freedom in the new independent Irish Free State.

After clashes between Protestant and Catholic residents, British soldiers were sent to patrol the streets of Belfast in 1969.

The Troubles

Decades of discrimination against the Catholic minority in Ulster sparked a civil rights movement in the 1960s. Badly handled by the Northern Irish Parliament and the largely Protestant security forces, the situation deteriorated into armed struggle. On Bloody Sunday in January 1972, thirteen demonstrators were killed. Northern Ireland erupted. On 21 July alone, twenty-two IRA bombs exploded in Belfast city centre. The Provisional IRA also carried the war to the British mainland, most famously by bombing the Brighton Grand Hotel during the Conservative Party

conference in 1984. Between 1969 and 2001, more than 3,500 people died in the Troubles. After several false starts, moves towards peace in the 1990s led to a ceasefire and resulted in the Belfast Agreement. This established an Executive and Parliament in Northern Ireland based upon power-sharing by the two communities.

Multicultural Britain

The arrival of immigrants after 1948 radically changed the ethnic make-up of British society.

After the Windrush

In 1948, 500 Jamaican immigrants disembarked from the SS *Empire Windrush* at Tilbury Docks in London. Many others from across the Commonwealth soon followed and the annual number of immigrants rose to over 100,000 in 1961. Although they were needed by Britain's changing economy, many experienced poor housing, low wages and public prejudice. In 1965, Labour passed the first Race Relations Act, making it illegal to refuse access to restaurants, hotels and pubs on grounds of race. Although the 'No Irish, No Blacks' signs came down from the windows of boarding houses, the act did little to stop discrimination against the newcomers.

Enoch Powell

In 1968, Labour introduced a second Race Relations Bill. The controversial Conservative MP Enoch Powell publicly attacked it, believing it would encourage immigrant communities 'to campaign against their fellow citizens' in demand of further

Jamaican immigrants arrive in Britain on the SS Empire Windrush *in 1948.*

In 2001, violent riots erupted in Bradford, Burnley and Oldham in the north of England, signalling the discontent in many ethnic communities.

special legal consideration. Powell's vivid speech caught the attention of the media and brought the question of mass immigration into public debate. While many attacked Powell as a racist, others believed the social disunity he predicted was borne out by race riots that erupted in the 1980s.

The Immigrant Experience

British immigrants experienced widely differing fortunes. Many West Indian nurses found rewarding careers in the National Health Service. Refugee Asians from East Africa arrived in Britain destitute, but quickly became leaders of British commerce. However, Asian workers who settled in the mill towns of northern England suffered as much as any other employee from the shrinking of Britain's manufacturing industry after 1970. Immigrants who could not speak good English and had poor skills often ended up in low-paid jobs and living in inner-city areas in Birmingham, Bradford, Leicester and Nottingham. By 2000 however, urban Britain had become a multiracial society on a scale unimaginable two generations before. Although many people of immigrant origin were rising to more prominent positions in British life, others felt they were victims of a deep-rooted prejudice, described as 'institutional racism'.

Multiculturalism?

Successive governments promoted the idea of multiculturalism, which offered equal status to all cultures in Britain. Critics feared the creation of ethnic ghettoes that would weaken national unity. Their fears seemed justified by the radicalization of elements within Britain's Muslim community after 2000. The suicide bombings of July 2005, in which four Muslim Englishmen murdered fifty-two commuters on the London Underground, forced many to think again about how to manage the problem of Britain's ethnic diversity. In 2006, the Labour government redefined British identity in terms of 'traditional values', such as history, tolerance and the rule of law, that were part of Britain's heritage.

Nationalism and Devolution

The merits of Scottish and Welsh Home Rule were debated from the 19th century onwards. A sense that Scotland and Wales were poorly governed led to a new Scottish Parliament and Welsh Assembly in 1999.

Home Rule for Scotland

The roots of modern Scottish nationalism lie in the disillusionment felt after World War I and during the years of economic slump. Many Scots increasingly felt that the British Parliament in Westminster neglected Scotland and that Scotland's economy suffered from union with England. In 1934, several nationalist groups merged into the Scottish National Party (SNP) but it made little impact at first. Instead, the Scottish Covenant Association kept the issue alive, collecting two million signatures in support of a Scottish Assembly in 1950.

Left to right: Dr Winnie Ewing, long-standing SNP representative, Alex Salmond, leader of the SNP, and actor and SNP supporter Sean Connery at the opening of the 1999 Scottish National Party Congress.

Scotland's Oil

In 1966 and 1967, Plaid Cymru (the National Party of Wales) and the SNP won by-elections at Carmarthen and Hamilton, both safe Labour seats. Labour had much to lose if the nationalists became popular in the industrialized areas of central Scotland and South Wales. This seemed possible, for the SNP won over 30 per cent of the Scottish vote and eleven Westminster seats in 1974. They were helped by the discovery of vast oil reserves under Scottish waters, which defused Labour's argument that Scotland could not afford to 'go it alone'. The Labour government offered referenda (votes on a single issue) for Scottish and Welsh assemblies in 1978 but although the majority of votes cast in Scotland were for an assembly, the proposal failed.

Convention and Parliament

Few Scots supported Prime Minister Thatcher, but Scotland's industries were badly affected by her policies. Scots deeply resented the closure of factories such as the Ravenscraig Steel Works in

Motherwell. In 1989, many Scottish politicians met with leading representatives of Scottish society to set up a constitutional convention that campaigned for devolution of powers to Scotland. In 1997, the New Labour government held referenda on its devolution plans. The 'Yes' campaign in Scotland received 75 per cent of the vote, although the referendum in Wales was much closer. Two years later, Winnie Ewing, the SNP victor at Hamilton in 1967, opened the first session of the Scottish Parliament since 1707.

West Lothian and Union

Devolution failed to address the 'West Lothian question' posed by the MP Tam Dalyell. After 1999, English MPs at Westminster lost all say over devolved issues such as education and health that were now Edinburgh's sole concern. Yet Scottish MPs at Westminster could still vote on these matters in an English context. Calls for Scottish MPs to withdraw from the Commons when English matters were being discussed were rejected by Labour, which depended on its Scottish members. Calls for an English Parliament grew louder in the press, and polls showed that many Scots and English were in favour of ending the union.

Timeline

1913	• Scottish Home Rule Bill postponed by WWI
1934	• Formation of the SNP
1945	• Election of the first SNP Member of Parliament
1974	• SNP wins over 30 per cent of the Scottish popular vote in a general election
1978	• Referenda for assemblies in Scotland and Wales produce no clear conclusion
1997	• Referenda in Scotland and Wales produce a 'Yes' vote for national assemblies
1999	• Opening of the Scottish Parliament and the Welsh Assembly

Queen Elizabeth visits Wales during celebrations for the opening of the Welsh Assembly in 1999.

1997–2007

The Age of Spin

In 1997, many people heralded the election of the first Labour government in eighteen years as a new dawn. But Prime Minister Tony Blair's New Labour project would run aground in the sands of Iraq.

New Labour

After 1979, Labour lost four consecutive elections, so in 1994 Tony Blair re-branded Labour to make it more electable. Labour leaders distanced themselves from the party's roots in trade unionism and socialism. Instead, they adopted market-orientated policies that acknowledged the realities of post-Thatcherite Britain. Blair's tight party management and careful attention to public presentation were criticized as 'control freakery' and 'spin'. However, New Labour easily defeated the Conservatives in 1997.

Things Can Only Get Better

Once in power, New Labour passed several important acts, such as the 1998 Human Rights Act and the Freedom of Information Act in 2000. A Scottish Parliament and Welsh Assembly were established, while the 1998 Belfast Agreement brought peace in Northern Ireland closer. However, the Millenium Dome, the symbol of Blair's 'Cool Britannia', was an expensive and unpopular flop. In Blair's second term the Ulster peace process stalled, while costly health service changes led to more NHS managers but little benefit for patients. At first, Chancellor Gordon Brown kept a tight control of public finances, but critics accused him of introducing 'stealth taxes' and questioned whether later increases in public spending had brought about real improvements to services.

Timeline

1994	• Tony Blair becomes Labour Party leader
1997	• Labour wins landslide general election victory
2001	• Blair wins second election
2002	• US government pushes for regime change in Iraq
August 2002	• Claim is made that Iraq can fire biological and chemical weapons within forty-five minutes
March 2003	• USA announces its intention to rid Iraq of 'weapons of mass destruction'
20 March 2003	• Largely US and UK coalition invades Iraq
September 2004	• Kofi Annan of the United Nations declares the war 'illegal'
2005	• Blair wins third general election
2005-2007	• Military and political situation in Iraq grows worse
2007	• Blair's popularity rating shows him as the least popular Prime Minister ever; he leaves office and is replaced by Gordon Brown

Iraq

In 2003, Blair followed the USA into war against the Iraqi dictator, Saddam Hussein. The Iraq war dominated the remainder of Blair's premiership. The legal justification for invading Iraq was weak and there was widespread public opposition to the war. Many MPs only accepted the decision to go to war because a government intelligence dossier claimed that the Iraqis could deploy weapons of mass destruction within forty-five minutes. Once it was established that the Iraqis had not possessed these weapons, Blair found it difficult to shake off the public perception of deceit. Saddam was easily overthrown in 2003 but the lack of a strategy for rebuilding Iraq led to chaos there. In December 2007, 4,500 British troops were still deployed in Iraq, and they had suffered 174 fatalities. Blair's credibility never recovered and he stood down in summer 2007.

20th-century Britain

Britain experienced great social and economic change in the 20th century. It had become more prosperous, especially after 1980, and was a fairer, more democratic society than in 1900. It had, however, lost its empire and was no longer a first-rank power. Many in Britain found it difficult to accept its new status as a medium-sized country that depended for influence on membership of the European Union. The rising tide of nationalism in all parts of Britain, including England, even raised the question of how long the United Kingdom of Great Britain and Northern Ireland could survive.

Three years after the invasion of Iraq, British troops continued to try to contain the violence and unrest that arose in the wake of Saddam Hussein's regime.

Glossary

annex to take over another country

apartheid racial segregation, as practised in South Africa for most of the 20th century

appeasement the policy of giving an enemy what he or she wants to avoid conflict

austerity lacking in comforts or luxuries

Boers members of the Dutch population who settled in South Africa from the 1700s

boycott refuse to buy or handle goods

by-election the election of an MP in a constituency to fill a vacancy arising during a government's term of office

census a survey, or count, of a population

charismatic having great personal qualities, such as energy and charm

coalition an alliance of different political parties usually in a government

Cold War period of tension between the Soviet Union and the Western Allies

colony a territory owned by another country, usually for trading

conscription the forced enlistment of men into the armed forces in wartime

convoy a group of ships travelling together, accompanied by warships for protection

democracy a country in which the people choose their own government

depression a serious slump in trade and economic activity

depth charge a device designed to explode underwater, used for attacking submarines

Dreadnought a class of warship that was fast, heavily armoured and well armed

fascism a militaristic political movement that first emerged in 1920s Italy

franchise the right to vote

guerrilla a soldier who ambushes the enemy instead of fighting him in large battles

hydrophone a microphone which detects sound waves underwater

inflation an increase in prices and fall in the purchasing value of money

International Monetary Fund (IMF) an agency that seeks to promote international co-operation on financial matters

means test a government check to see if families really needed financial help

militant very active in support of a cause

munitions weapons and ammunition

national insurance money paid by the government to the sick to avoid hardship

nationalist someone who wants his or her country to be independent and govern itself

pension money payments made to the retired and elderly

picket a group that stands outside a place of work to protest and try to persuade employees or clients from entering

privatize to sell off government-run industries to private investors

propaganda messages to persuade people to support a particular point of view

radical in favour of social or political reform

sanctions measures taken by one country to enforce obedience by another

sonar a system for detecting objects underwater through the use of sound waves

stalemate the inability of either side in a war to gain an outright victory

suffrage the right to vote

trade union an association of workers, formed to protect and further their rights

trench-foot a gangrenous condition suffered by soldiers in wet trenches

welfare state the redistribution of wealth through taxes to help every citizen of country

Timeline

1903	• Formation of the WSPU (Women's Social & Political Union)
1906	• Liberals win election victory and create the welfare state
1909	• Lloyd George introduces the old age pension
1911	• Parliament Act makes Commons more powerful than the Lords
1914	• Britain enters World War I
1918	• Limited franchise given to women over the age of thirty
1922	• Ireland divided into southern Free State and Protestant north
1926	• The General Strike
1930-35	• The Great Depression
1938	• Chamberlain tries to prevent war by appeasing Hitler at Munich
1939	• Britain enters World War II after Germany invades Poland
1940	• RAF defeats the German Luftwaffe in the Battle of Britain
1942	• British victory in North Africa signals turning point in the war
1945	• The Allies finally achieve victory over Nazi Germany and Japan
1945-51	• Labour extends the welfare state
1947	• British withdraw from India
1951-70	• Rise of the consumer society
1957	• Britain humiliated in Suez Crisis
1968	• Enoch Powell makes his controversial speech about immigration
1972	• Bloody Sunday in Ireland
1973	• Britain joins EEC
1979-90	• Thatcher crushes trade union power and reinvigorates the economy
1998	• Belfast Agreement increases the chance of peace in Northern Ireland
1999	• Establishment of new Scottish Parliament and Welsh Assembly
2003	• Britain sends troops to assist the USA in the invasion of Iraq

Further Information

Books

Picture History of the 20th Century: 1900-1919, Richard Tames, Franklin Watts, 2004

The First World War, Dennis Hamley, Franklin Watts, 2005

World War Two Britain: History From Buildings, Stewart Ross, Franklin Watts, 2006

Twentieth Century History Makers: Winston Churchill, Simon Adams, Franklin Watts, 2006

Scotland Since 1900, Richard Dargie, Heinemann, 2001

Websites

http://www.britannia.com/history/h90.html
lists of key figures and events

http://www.britannia.com/history/nar20hist.html
detailed textual narrative of the history of Britain in clear chapters

http://www.bbc.co.uk/history/british/modern/jmurray_01.shtml
well written and readable history of British women throughout the 20th century

http://www.bbc.co.uk/history/british/modern/
excellent treatment of key topics in British history since 1945

http://www.britishempire.co.uk/timeline/20century.htm
timeline of key events relating to Britain and its empire since 1900

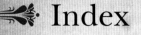

Index